RUINS

MARY BURRITT CHRISTIANSEN POETRY SERIES

V. B. PRICE, SERIES EDITOR

Mary Burritt
Christiansen
Poetry Series

Also available in the University of New Mexico Press
Mary Burritt Christiansen Poetry Series:

Poets of the Non-Existent City: Los Angeles in the McCarthy Era edited by
Estelle Gershgoren Novak

Selected Poems of Gabriela Mistral edited by Ursula K. Le Guin

Deeply Dug In by R. L. Barth

Amulet Songs: Poems Selected and New by Lucile Adler

In Company: An Anthology of New Mexico Poets After 1960 edited by Lee
Bartlett, V. B. Price, and Dianne Edenfield Edwards

Tiempos Lejanos: Poetic Images from the Past by Nasario García

Refuge of Whirling Light by Mary Beath

*The River Is Wide/El río es ancho: Twenty Mexican Poets, a Bilingual
Anthology* edited and translated by Marlon L. Fick

A Scar Upon Our Voice by Robin Coffee

CrashBoomLove: A Novel in Verse by Juan Felipe Herrera

In a Dybbuk's Raincoat: Collected Poems by Bert Meyers

Rebirth of Wonder: Poems of the Common Life by
David M. Johnson

Broken and Reset: Selected Poems, 1966 to 2006 by V. B. Price

The Curvature of the Earth by Gene Frumkin and
Alvaro Cardona-Hine

Derivative of the Moving Image by Jennifer Bartlett

Map of the Lost by Miriam Sagan

¿de Veras?: Young Voices from the National Hispanic Cultural Center
edited by Mikaela Jae Renz and Shelle VanEtten-Luaces

*A Bigger Boat: The Unlikely Success of the Albuquerque Poetry Slam
Scene* edited by Susan McAllister, Don McIver, Mikaela Renz, and
Daniel S. Solis

A Poetry of Remembrance: New and Rejected Works by Levi Romero

The Welcome Table by Jay Udall

How Shadows Are Bundled by Anne Valley-Fox

Bolitas de oro: Poems of My Marble-Playing Days by Nasario García

Blood Desert: Witnesses, 1820–1880 by Renny Golden

The Singing Bowl by Joan Logghe

Begging for Vultures by Lawrence Welsh

RUINS

〜

Margaret Randall

FOREWORD BY V. B. PRICE

UNIVERSITY OF NEW MEXICO PRESS

ALBUQUERQUE

© 2011 by the University of New Mexico Press
All rights reserved. Published 2011
Printed in the United States of America
15 14 13 12 11   1 2 3 4 5

Library of Congress Cataloging-in-Publication Data

Randall, Margaret, 1936–
  Ruins / Margaret Randall ; foreword by V. B. Price.
      p. cm. — (Mary Burritt Christiansen poetry series)
  Includes bibliographical references.
  ISBN 978-0-8263-5067-1 (pbk. : alk. paper) — ISBN 978-0-8263-5068-8
(electronic)
  I. Title.
  PS3535.A56277R85 2011
  811'.54—dc22
                              2011010689

for Barbara:
my artist, my love.

CONTENTS

ᔕ FOREWORD

Hardly anything escapes the tenderness and uncensored candor of Margaret Randall's curiosity. In her latest book of poems, *Ruins*, Randall opens herself empathetically to time's perpetual undoing and what it leaves behind. Like the Anglo-Saxon poets of "The Wanderer" and "The Seafarer," Randall absorbs the remains of the past that age "underate." Because she lives her life wide open and full out, her poems have an elevating intimacy with the flow of loss and its inevitable pain as it piles up behind the future. She uses the metaphor of ruins to meditate on what's left behind and what it means as time moves through memory, through cities, through the leavings of history, and through the bodies of lives who have experienced time's transformations and traumas.

A poet and writer of impeccable integrity and unwavering social conscience, Randall has spent much of her life outside the United States supporting humane causes and human rights in Mexico, Cuba, Nicaragua, Vietnam, and Peru. When she returned to the United States in 1984, the federal government tried to deport her for her political opinions. She won a five-year legal struggle and now lives in New Mexico where she grew up.

The poems here stretch the sense of ruins to include not only Chaco Canyon, Hovenweep, Teotihuácan,[1] Machu Picchu, Kiet Siel, Petra, and sites in ancient Greece and Egypt, but also the design documents of Auschwitz-Birkenau and the living ruins of lives shattered by torture and oppression. This wider view of ruins includes the ruins of our own minds, fragmentary memories eroding like landscapes, ruins of history as they exist as parts of our internalized experience. Choosing to live her life as both an appreciator and a worker for social justice allows Randall to infuse these ruins with the intensity of her receptiveness. Using metaphors so personal that they become universal helps us to expand our lives into the lives and times of others, to liberate ourselves from the present and exist for a moment in the freedom of the timeless.

In "Survivor," Randall writes of a single tree in Pueblo Bonito, the major ruin of Chaco Canyon in northwest New Mexico. This tree was a

> cosmic point marking past, present, and future
> in temporal dimension,
> lower, middle, and upper worlds
> on a map we hold uneasily.
>
> . . . the stump of a great pine
> insists it is axis, one more in a range of clues
> that tell us more than we ought to know.
> Is the great house also a sundial,
> claiming the passage of time?

In the ruins of her lifetime, Randall writes of Nazi architectural drawings enshrined in Israel as proof of the Holocaust in "Evidence":

> No blueprints of Palestinian homes
> beckon the curious or devout
> here or anywhere.
> No memorial
> keeps them under glass,
> providing evidence to the world
> of lives raised, shattered,
> and raised again.

Randall's intuitive familiarity with the borders between now, the future it was, and the past it will always be is brought to life in her homage to Hermes, god of travelers and borders, of interpretation and messages from the powers that be, and the guide of the dead.

"Hermes, Shapeshifter" is the perfect Orphic poem, in which the poet loses love by second-guessing the present as it falls away into the past, a nonworld in which loss exists in

> Liminal space: threshold between Here and There,
> even when Here retreats
> into the silver-grey of early morning light
> and There turns her back
> as you reach and grab her hand.

> . . . Hermes slips between tectonic plates,
> balancing a present that disappears

> and a future never quite brought to focus,
> pulls us
> between one last burst of rage
> and the perfect halves
> of this geode opening to our touch.

In "Blood Lightning Speaks," Randall's perfect ear hears the sound of time running through stone calendars in the jungles of the Maya where

> Blood lightning speaks and stars dip
> to that mindful sea
> as great kettles of hawks funnel south
> and each stalk of corn
> turns to its left and bows.

> Keeping up with the sun, stalks rise,
> guided by stars and birds:

cause and effect interchangeable
in a place where sky instructs
and time holds past and future

in a single breath.

As a poet and philosopher, Margaret Randall masterfully focuses poetry into an instrument of perception, a means of seeing and understanding realities that exist almost beyond the borders of language. The poems in *Ruins* live in that realm where empathy can see what reason cannot, and where poetry can say the truth within the lost spaces of the facts that disappeared, replaced by Orphic presence like an ancient seashell is replaced by stone, exactly as it was but no longer is.

—V. B. Price, Albuquerque

PREFACE 〜 *An Arrival*

For many years I have been drawn to ancient ruins, sites where everything is different but one can still perceive the architecture of community. Landscape, climate, culture, and the passage of time make each of these places unique. Whether what remains stands awesome in great amphitheaters, columns, and facades, or is barely suggested beneath the proud shoulders of unexcavated land, I am transfixed. Hearing Santa Clara scholar and environmentalist Rina Swentzell say, "If you think of the sky as the roof of your house, everything is intimate," introduced me to a new way of perceiving places where those who came before us passed or took up residence.

Always there is that moment of arrival as another reality rises before me, superimposed upon the one I live today. Sometimes the membrane is torn, and I find myself moving in and out. Boundaries dissolve. A mysterious space between Then and Now warns as it invites, promising revelation and maybe also fresh trauma, if I am willing to risk its secrets.

Perhaps I've seen pictures or formed expectations from what others have said (although I do some reading before a first visit, I tend to do much more afterward—my deepest research invariably takes place once I have internalized the site's contours, circularity, voice). Whatever the preparation, nothing can rob that initial moment of its astonishing richness. Weather. Time. Company. No matter the day or situation, wherever and whenever an ancient ruin reveals itself it becomes a part of who I am.

I do not have to actively imagine what life may have been like when what remains was a thriving community or major metropolis. The experience is more holistic; it occurs as if by osmosis. The people themselves come to me. With neither astonishment nor ritual they appear, beckoning me to accompany them in their mundane occupations. And these are not throngs but individuals. Spirits? I wouldn't want to hazard a guess. Suffice it to say that some dimension is breached: the skin of time and linear history, a shape-shifting of energy, memory's direction, the knowledge that tells us less is more.

Perhaps we will cook together. Or philosophize about issues we cannot yet know were settled many centuries later. Although I gravitate more toward women, I have noticed that gender is largely irrelevant in my experience of these places: race, class, age, sexuality, who people are in all their manifestations, dissolve along great arcs of identity—much as they do today but less burdened by socially prescribed and judgment-laden labels. I am as likely to find myself conversing with Socrates as we walk through Athens's marketplace as grinding corn with other women in an alcove on the Colorado Plateau. Dates become maps upon which the intersections of longitudinal and latitudinal lines speak in rich complexity.

Sometimes I discover the ancient in places where no ruins stand. Borders, walls, and fences scar the earth, in ways trapping lives that might have been, exposing unfinished dreams. Death, too, startles us into seeing or feeling beyond experiences easily understood.

One constant is art. Or what we, in our compartmentalized society, have taken to calling art. The chewed yucca-strand brush used to decorate slip on a Mogollon pot settles between the fingers of my right hand, or perhaps my left. A bare sole carved into rock has six toes; was this my child's foot? Did the extra appendage speak of deformity or magical power? I stand back to view the big-horned sheep I have just chipped into an Escalante Canyon wall. The weight of the stone chisel with which I pecked away at an Inca rock slab balances between hand and wrist; others, stronger than me, carried the great stones and fitted them in patterned grandeur.

Spinning and weaving also pull me into their orb, gold and precious stones delight my love of beauty as a realm of its own. Do I know if this small spiral etched on a canyon wall denotes a place where water waits or records a moment of celestial explosion? I don't believe these ancient images were subject to our whims of status and marketplace, but I cannot know what place they held in cultures as distant in time and space as seas parched to desert sands. When sudden death stops an artist's seeing, what happens to the gaze's energy?

Other constants are need and greed, peace and congeniality. How do we move forward in exploration and discovery without trampling the rights of others to do the same? How is difference viewed: with appreciation or self-righteous intolerance? What rules can we evolve or customs observe to make sure the bounty of this land shelters and feeds and clothes us all, meeting material requirements as well as giving us time to think and make, to develop the ideas others after us will build upon?

I am looking for past, and also for present and future in the past. It is easy to believe today that there has never been a time so grave, so dangerous to the earth and life's continuance. That environmental disaster is upon us, and what we don't destroy with greenhouse gas, we will obliterate with rootlessness, famine, war, and the smaller, more intimate acts of cruelty.

I imagine that peoples of every time and place have judged the threats to their survival as dramatic, felt pressed upon to devise solutions to the problems they faced, and felt desperate when they failed. Loneliness, loss, hunger, heartache, fire, and flood can and do strike at any time. The anguish felt by those trapped by the wall of lava at Pompeii cannot have been that different from the anguish experienced by those caught in the cascading buildings of Port-au-Prince.

Mine are not casual field trips. Something mysterious yet ordinary draws me to these sites, whether in the deep Central American jungles or tourist-filled kingdoms of ancient Egypt, in the hidden alcoves of my own U.S. Southwest or in the Golden Proportion of Greece's perfect columns, gazing at a Hittite water temple set among wheat fields in Turkey's high country, or tracing the twin silhouettes of mountains and hand-placed rock on the rain-soaked saddle of Machu Picchu.

Again and again I am home.

Given this propensity, it's not surprising that at some point these poems would emerge in series, as a book. Ruins or other evidence of ancient community are prominent in much of my earlier writing. I have made hundreds of photographic images of these places as well. Yet this time around, when I began writing, I naïvely believed I was producing one discrete poem and then another. I had recently completed *My Town*, a collection about growing up in Albuquerque in the 1940s and 1950s. Before that, I had published another single-themed volume: *Their Backs to the Sea*, which had its origins in Easter Island. I was actually happy to be exploring what I believed to be more diverse subject matter.

Except I soon discovered this wasn't the case. And the sites of ancient life—as culturally, physically, and geographically diverse as concentrations of people throughout time—provided a palette as broad as it is rich. One after another, poems rooted in ruins appeared on my computer monitor and then on the printed page.

Once again I strolled between the high walls of Petra's Siq to emerge, startled despite every guidebook preview, when it parted to reveal the carved pink rock of The Treasury. Or rode beside Barbara as we drove along a back road in southern Utah and I happened to look up and spot a small Ancestral Puebloan ruin tucked into the side of a cliff; or was caught in a sudden desert hailstorm as we hiked to Horseshoe Canyon's Great Gallery. Again I walked through the dense jungle at Cobá in southern Mexico, imagining what lay beneath mounds still overgrown with sod and root. Listened to the roar of the howlers as I made my way along a narrow path at Tikal, then gasped as I caught sight of the first tall pyramid rising above the trees. Or stood quietly among the fallen stone and broken clay pipes of Turkey's Perga, imagining my body being washed by the healing waters of its baths.

My mind and sensibility raced back and forth between these images and the issues that have long concerned me—justice, power, memory, struggle, survival, violence, greed, love, and the role of art. These poems are rooted in ancient sites but—as is true of most of my work—are not content with simple description. There is always dichotomy and counterpoint between the holographic image of what was and the equally holographic image of what might be. Traces of human landscape speak to me of what is possible.

Once I understood what was happening, the poems literally tumbled out. I woke at two or three in the morning, unable to stay in bed; so strong was my need to write. Images and feelings flooded me, overpowering in their gravitational force. Sometimes I drafted two or three poems in a single day, although it took the wisdom of time to reshape them as they now appear.

I am deeply indebted to poet, anthropologist, and critic V. B. Price, whose own engagement with ancient places and their myths recognized mine. His work sings to me, and his shepherding of this book has been a very special gift. I am also and always grateful to my partner Barbara for her close reading of every line; having accompanied me to most of these places, she was particularly astute in her attention to my rendering.

Places We Call Home

This is the center, the great hub,
its spokes moving arrow-straight
to the cardinal directions.
Roads wide as runways,
perhaps more for ritual than travel
to a thousand outlier communities,
north as far as Betatakin and Kiet Siel,
south to Paquimé.

The Great Houses stand either side
of this broad wash, under hovering cliffs
and sky that is always blue
even when roiling clouds
bulk before releasing
infrequent rain.
On the desert water can kill
as surely as it saves.

Pueblo Bonito, Chetro Ketl, Kin Kletso,
Pueblo Alto and Casa Rinconada:
names that inhabit the mouth
or slip off the tongue
from early inhabitants, explorers
and scholars, sometimes
reflecting what happened here
and sometimes not.

Shimmying up the long fracture of rock
above Pueblo Bonito
my camera pack catches in the narrow crack.
I turn to free myself

and move to where I look down
on the half-moon like a scale model
its tiny figures appearing
and disappearing room to room.

I have come here with the woman
I love, intending to camp
then dissuaded by mosquitoes.
With grandchildren I must convince
to leave broken pottery where it lies.
Friends who suffer in the midday heat
or cannot still
their racing hearts.

Each visit I look for the mountain lion:
tiny petroglyph figure on the cliff
that borders a trail
linking one great house with another.
Each visit I run my hand
the length of Chetro Ketl's wall,
ponder its array of kivas
or strain to glimpse the Moqui steps I'll never climb.

January 22, 1941: I was four years old
when thirty thousand tons of rock
fractured and fell on Pueblo Bonito,
destroying its north wall
and sixty-five rooms. What other
Chaco dates weave in and out
of mine, before, during

or beyond my passage?
There will always be a next time
I tell myself, another visit
to contemplate Wetherill's shame
or learn about the 18.2-year intervals
when earth and sky align
and a sliver of light
descends a wall,
changing the course of history.

Here swallows nest in little pockets of mud
on sandstone walls that drip
with desert varnish,
petroglyphs bear rude bullet holes,
each season picks up
where the one before it vanished,
and the sun always keeps
its promise to itself.

Maybe I lived here once or visited
from north or south.
Maybe the tiny turquoise bead
you placed in my hand
is from a string I wore
eight hundred years ago.
Maybe we all return
to the places we call home.

Survivor

for my daughter Ana

Tree of Life, lone survivor of ancient forest
or gnomon—found or planted—
cosmic point marking past, present, and future
in temporal dimension,
lower, middle, and upper worlds
on a map we hold uneasily.

Anchoring Pueblo Bonito's west plaza,
the stump of a great pine
insists it is axis, one more in a range of clues
that tell us more than we ought to know.
Is the great house also a sundial
claiming the passage of time?

Will this tree invite us to touch its roots,
hear the muted story
of its sun-bleached rings?

Carrying Dead Mothers at Our Breast
for Janine Pommy Vega

You enter the room and I begin to remember
a half-century folds its arms across my chest
like your dream of a daughter
gathering her murdered mother's arms and legs
into some ancient burial bundle,
tying the body like a package to her breast
then covering it with a loose blouse
as if pregnant
and walking, walking.

Walking with bones and desiccating flesh
in search of somewhere, a safe place
we want to believe exists
beyond our pleated hope.
Walking out of New Jersey,
a planet unto itself: 1960 or '61,
image of you slim in a peasant skirt,
vague pattern of red.

You were 16, maybe 17, I 21 or 22,
my son still unimagined
in my desire.
Back then it was your lean young husband
made the impression
and now you tell me he died at 33,
heroin spike in his arm,
Lorca as witness and company.

We were young women in a world
that hated women
unless we stood up fast
or clawed our way
through groin to consciousness.
You had the hard drugs
which may have made it easier.
I was already headed south.

Now we are two aging sisters,
unruly still, clear eyed,
loud and speaking our visions
to the world,
keeping our dead close to these bodies,
the skirts we wore back then
flailing in some parallel universe.

You twisted by rheumatoid arthritis,
knots of bone that prove no match
for your dance.
I missing a kidney, my lungs caged
in their own sordid history,
and we keep on walking, walking,
haciendo camino al andar,
the poet said.

Your dream woman and her mother's bones
find safety in a house at travel's end,
just as you and I
inhabit explosions of place and language
where everything happens:
cultures that give us questions
and sometimes answers.

Until we learn expectation itself is the culprit,
liquid that drowns passion
crows victory before eyes fly open
or magic settles in pores
and the final challenge holds memory
up to a brighter light, chooses
which doors to close and which
to keep on walking through.

I didn't really know you back then
but with your lesson in walking
histories converge
along some point on the curve:
distant as other lives
close as the pain of moving forward
carrying dead mothers at our breast.

Chocolate Zigzags[2]
for Roxanne Dunbar-Ortíz

Chocolate zigzags through my blood,
chromatic blue-grey on white
or white against dark slate
geometry of those cylindrical mugs
tasting of moments at Pueblo Bonito
and the Mayan kingdoms
thousands of miles south.

Unique drinking vessels
not found at burial sites
but in places of community
where rites of passage
still exude cacao pungency:
seeds ground with water,
spiked with corn and chile pepper fire.

At Pueblo Bonito traces of Theobromine
live on in ancient clay,
revealing their heady tale.
At Chichén and Palenque
a young woman in first blood
runs her tongue along the froth
lighting her veins,

a young man stands on the bridge
of marriage, war, or death:
defining journey of his life.
Age too has its ceremonies
our chemical tests
cannot determine,
weathered skin licked mystery-clean.

Ghosts walk two thousand miles
of curiosity and trade,
offer live scarlet macaws,
copper bells, and this exquisite taste
called Hershey or Godiva today
empty of ritual or vessel
beyond the ribbons of its cushioned box.

The ancient aphrodisiac endangers
and comforts simultaneously,
holds our hands in times of grief
keeps us from dwelling
on our friend three years gone,
whose discovered death
now tears me limb from limb.

Nankoweap

At Nankoweap, fifteen hundred feet
above the broad delta
where burnt tamarisk branches keen
early morning light
and tree frogs croak their broken song,
a row of windowed rooms
lures the apex of vertical ascent.

Granaries: storehouses
where grain would be safe
through long winters
and times of drought,
usually built high and to the back
of dwellings and ceremonial spaces
in the alcoves that beckon us.

Bits of scree loosen beneath my feet,
skittering down the steep incline
where I put one frightened boot
before the other, look to my guide
for encouragement,
will myself to move forward,
claim victory on my first such climb.

On a narrow ledge just below the ruin
I struggle to find purchase, a place
to sit and rest, turn my body
and marvel at these perfect enclosures
—I can almost touch them now—
their slab doors hiding
more than I am taught to know.

Here, at Mile 52 of the Colorado,
where Marble Canyon spreads
its fan of oranges, reds,
rose pinks and purples,
the river snake glistens silver blue
as it turns and disappears,
eaten by distant buttes.

Before me: alert days, velvet nights
of brilliant stars. Geology. History. Silence.
Behind me: first knowledge
my feet can ascend perpendicular rock
to a place where people like ourselves
solved problems of sustenance,
frugality and greed.

Hovenweep

Finely made stone towers, some four stories tall,
rise out of narrow box canyons
straddling the Colorado-Utah border.
Easy to access though guidebooks still warn
of miles of rough dirt track.

We have often been drawn to Hovenweep
"Deserted Valley" the ancients called this place,
but two visits stand tall as its towers in memory.
And drawn is not a word I dispatch
or utter casually.

Pulled as if by magnet force, I breathe hard
until we land in the small parking lot
by the visitor center,
only recently replacing the wooden shack
that was its predecessor.

Horizon's circle brings flat desert into view
and the eye moves out
to Arizona's Carrizo peaks, Utah's La Sals
or the closer hulk of Sleeping Ute,
resting west of Mesa Verde.

We arrive via Blanding or McElmo Canyon
through rabbitbrush, low sage,
occasional cattail and twisted piñon,
the milkweed and beewood
those who lived here took for food.

Juniper gnats throw a mean sting.
Bright aqua collared lizards
—each a tiny Priscilla, Queen of the Desert—
do impressive push-ups, their luminescence
yellow/blue/green in the scorching sun.

Those who built these towers settled in a place
where nomads traveled ten thousand years before.
A community, thriving in AD 900
vanished in 1250,
leaving only deer and cottontail.

What remains—oval, square, and D-shaped structures
built on foundations of fallen rimrock
where sandstone platforms
and carefully laid tiers of cut stone
function in perfect tandem—may have been

for astronomical observation, signaling across
great distances, storage, or defense.
One curious ruin nestles within the jaws
of a great rock mouth.
Scholars do not speak of dwelling.

The first of the two visits we're with Mother:
in her eighties then, small and fragile
but grateful for the chance
to know the magic of this place.
You remove the straps from your pack

and fashion a makeshift belt to hold her steady,
walking backwards before her,
navigating the two-mile trail,
pausing often so she can catch her breath,
the three of us radiant in discovery.

In my other memory we are alone, alone
and together in these places
that feed the spirit. Perhaps, we think,
we will retrace known routes or hike
to one of the outliers.

As we lock the car and turn
toward whatever the morning brings,
a heavyset older man in familiar ranger uniform
emerges from the visitor center,
walking stick in hand.

On time for the 10 a.m. he smiles at no one
but us. *We want to see the rock art
we've searched for but never found.*
He nods and the three of us set out,
descending slowly to the shallow canyon floor.

Mostly in silence we wind along trails
he's made his own. Then he raises his staff
and points to the sheltered side
of a free-standing boulder
we would have missed without his eye.

Under its narrow overhang,
one tight spiral pecked in the surface
unwinds toward a single human figure.
Higher and to the right, another line
stair-steps, geometric as it climbs the rock.

Minutes further, at the back wall of a cave
we must stoop to enter,
several red handprints fade
against a surface of ochre stone.
No one speaks. Centuries contract.

I smell red lichen on sunbaked rock.
A collared lizard basks and pants.
Hovenweep pulls us back,
its very name a source of power,
the mysterious towers defiant in my eyes.

I am the artist. My hand still traces
their contours
on overlapping folds of time.

Kiet Siel
for Mark Behr

Almost too late you say let's go,
you'll carry sixty or seventy pounds
to my twenty, urge me to make
the reservation: between
May and September they let
twenty hikers in a day.

I study maps, consider spring rains
and what I will prepare for us to eat.
Keep it light, I think,
my heart already racing
toward that place where one giant pine
kept people in or out.

Eighteen half-mile markers lead us
through shifting sand,
animal tracks and wildflowers
coax us on.
Kiet Siel stands as it has for centuries
in its alcove above the delta.

Strange to think of delta in this desert,
but the river that threatens us
with quicksand
would have been bigger then,
feeding patches of corn and beans,
wetting the pinched lips of clay pots.

It is those pots, some of them broken
but placed where they might have been,
those pots and corncobs cleaned of kernels

that lure us where we imagine
a man lifting a beam, a woman grinding,
a child turning her face to ours.

On tough hikes there is always
that moment I must complain
I can't go on. Stop. Breathe.
Loosen the straps constraining
shoulders and will.
Then stand and proceed without another word.

Always a second breath,
fuller than the first,
ready to carry me through
as I move ahead,
walking in front of you now,
lulled by the thud of heavy boots.

When we reach the stand of Gambel oak
and tiny campsite,
we know the ruin can't be far,
leave our packs,
stretch aching bodies,
and ford one last creek crossing,

hurrying to wait before the hogan gate,
coughing in the Navajo way of saying
we are here, until a young man
emerges to take us through
a final spread of undergrowth
where spirits wait.

And there they are, as eight hundred years ago,
when men and women worked
and children played
on the broad avenue
that fronts the complex
of kivas, rooms and walls.

Who knew we would have to climb
an almost vertical seventy-foot ladder
to enter our destination?
We exchange a look
but drip cold sweat
and meet the challenge wordlessly.

Precious hours walking from room
to room, tracing painted turkeys
with our eyes, imagining bright macaws
squawking from poles that rise
beside perfect windows, doors
barely tall enough to let a body through.

Time slows then stops
as the Navajo caretaker tells us
why his grandfather
didn't want him to take this job,
disturb the spirits
who still reside within these walls.

That night we watch from camp
as shadows fill the space
where Kiet Siel is or was,
warm ourselves
in the solar-powered pit toilet
before taking off at dawn.
The return is lighter and faster

as we check off features of the land
and retrieve stashed water bottles,
the people of the delta
and their habitat
homesteading in our eyes.

Before They Changed the Rules

1.

One more Ancestral Puebloan site
where we may no longer sit quietly,
careful not to lean
against her fragile walls,
respectful of her silences.
Long afternoon shadows
draw dark stripes
down Betatakin's alcove
we can only contemplate
except from a distance.
The prudent ranger will take us
within five hundred feet.

I remember the guide who led us in
before they changed the rules.
He walked fast, too fast for me,
until I understood
he wouldn't leave me behind
and slowed my pace, breathing again.
The man answered each question:
The Hopi say it happened this way,
anthropologists say something else,
but we Navajos know . . .
only the faintest smile
lighting his triple response.

He shared his grandmother's story:
They hid three years
in those mountains over there
to escape the government troops
when they rounded us up
for the march to Bosque Redondo.

That's when his words
rose in pitch
and he used the plural *us*
though he wasn't born
when his people endured the travesty
running in his veins today.

2.

In my breast there will always be
a cluster of impatient cells
where the caves of Lascaux
wait expectantly.
Their horses, bison, and bulls run
between gestures of yellow, red, black,
and those stone walls.
I wasn't yet 30 when carbon dioxide
closed them to a public
I didn't know included me.
Black mold sealed my fate,
and there was no way home.

Those artists didn't paint
their surroundings
back then:
not a single reindeer
on those walls,
though that was their meat of choice.
There's only imagination's power
and forty thousand years
I will never bridge
because a million visitors
breathed too hard
and mold beat me to the draw.

3.
I am doing my best
not to mourn Lascaux
but be grateful
I made it to Betatakin in time.

Chosen or Imposed

Several days' walk from the silent ruin,
this single dwelling hides
around a canyon bend.
Same snug walls, same evidence
of cooking smoke on stone
and high storage bins
where ladders, long erased
by time and weather,
rose to winter sustenance.

I want to know who the outcasts were
and if they were sent away
or chose to live apart.
Was it discord, rivalry,
disease or love of solitude
forced or lured
those who inhabited
this place so distant
from community's embrace?

Today color, religious conduct,
politics, who we love
and what locks we use
to keep others from our door
are reasons for separation—
chosen or imposed.
Could urban planning
in our ancestors' time
have been as unimaginative?

I Happened to Look Out My Window

It might have been just before we took the Burr Trail
or some point along that latitude of southern Utah
north of the waters that destroyed Glen Canyon,
receding now with each corroding drought,
delighting those who mourn her drowned secrets.

You were driving. I happened to look out my window
and there, not five hundred feet from the road,
clenched against the red rock face
were three or four small rooms, neatly layered stone,
wattled windows and keyhole doors:

home to Ancestral Puebloans. We stopped and
climbed to the ledge where further details
met us in mid-morning sun: rows of tiny stones
between the larger blocks, a rounded corner,
a single shoeprint preceding us in discovery.

For days we looked at maps, in books, inquired
of those we thought might know the small ruin.
Did it have a name, given in that time or this?
Following the same route back, alert
to its gifts, always looking up, we saw nothing.

So many ancient homesteads dot that landscape,
charge entrance fees to tourists
or hide beneath the sand and sod
with stories our children and grandchildren will learn
when they decipher their pieces of the puzzle.

What's one more? Nothing larger or smaller
than home and precious community
to those who lived in its consecrated space,
and we who feel their presence, stone by stone:
a bridge from their time to our own.

Tanka

Evening slickrock stage
you raise your grandmother flute
to lips and fingers
sweet notes invade broken walls
ancient ones turn and listen

Brazil Is the First to Fade

Tuvalu and Tonga, Kiribati, the Maldives
and Cape Verde
have warned us they will die.
Noah's Ark in reverse,
nations two by two falling
over themselves, sinking from sight.

Nothing less than salvation
is ordered.
We sit around a large table,
crisis choking every throat.
I look at my comrades,
then at the spread of maps.

Brazil is the first to fade
from South America's proud terrain,
its whole northwest
leaving a giant sinkhole
in the middle of the continent.
Australia and Greenland: both gone.

I catch sight of a free South Africa
just as it slips beneath the sea,
mountains and streams
broken and scattered,
a township of children waving
as they disappear.

We will be next, so I cannot hold
to our shameful habit of relief:
always another's gaping eyes

or swollen belly,
another's hacked limbs,
endless line of wanderers

willing one foot before the other.
The dream cuts my stalk
to the ground,
threatens its bravest roots:
a warning I hold in hands
that grip the bedsheets as I wake.

Today It Is Haiti

Contrasting man-made tragedies
with natural disasters,
easy labels
defy the laws of gravity.
A difference that tells us nothing
about what happened
or why.

Today it is Haiti. Seven-point earthquake
leaving thousands dead or dying.
A woman's broken body
draped over a wheelbarrow.
Natural disaster, say those who give the news,
fade human-created slums
to blood and memory.

Yesterday it was Khao Lak, the Gulf Coast,
Darfur, Rwanda,
and other human landscapes:
a levee that cannot hold,
sudden tremor, mad hordes
washing bodies out to sea
or hacking them apart on land.

Those we assign to poverty
are forever vulnerable
to God's punishing hand.

Offended Turf
for Glenn Weyant

I press my face against dark steel tubes,
fourteen feet high,
filled with poured concrete
solid as fear,
undulating over these rises and hollows
of desecrated land,
like the Great Wall of China
without its invitation to walk.

We are making music here,
you with your cello bow,
percussion implements
and contact mike.
Me with words I coax
from walls and fences everywhere.
We are taking a chance our vibrations
will change these molecules of hate.

Along this fictitious border
dark tubes snake,
throwing their shadows in foreshortened stripes
across offended turf
until they stop, suddenly,
beyond washes threatening our vehicle.
Two Border Patrol SUVs race to the far end,
intent on beating us to the unprotected crossing.

Government calls this a fence
though it's clearly a wall,
its solid dimension
meant to keep humans, small animals,

and cultures apart.
Between uprights I glimpse the old mattress springs
and sad ocotillo laced with barbed wire,
irrelevant in sand.

Closer to Nogales—Charlie Mingus's town,
where neither statue nor street name
honor his passionate bass—
the wall is makeshift patches
of battered war matériel,
weathered and graffitied
with little doors
not for human passage but the same patrol of men

in dark green uniforms and white SUVs
with green stripes—
as if bringing green
to this improbable equation
will give an illusion of life.
The officers warn us against stones
thrown from the other side.
Some sport cages on their moving arsenals.

Standing by a Wackenhut bus
waiting to fill with the unsuccessful
it will deliver to the other side,
guards wear gunmetal grey
with red and black insignias:
fascism, empty power
aimed at the most vulnerable.
Aimed at us all.

Along the lonely desert roads
with clusters of Minutemen
in unmarked cars,
a parade of jeeps
with license plates from far-flung states
abandon plastic gallon jugs,
some filled with the urine of desperation,
some cracked beneath mid-March sun.

This month's heat is no match for July
or August, yet brittle earth
cradles the dead
on a landscape of mesquite and ironwood,
cacti and rabbitbrush,
where one nameless cross
wails INRI and *adios*
to all who pass.

At Arivaca we stop at a small café
for coffee and pie. A group of bikers talk
beneath the shade of improbable trees.
On the walls: flyers for "No More Deaths"
recognize locals
who organize a first line of defense
for those who only want to live.

Surrounded by virtual fence towers
—billions spent on failure—
dry ocotillo, barbed wire,
rusted mattress springs,
patched metal from every war
and imposing cement-filled tubes,
we have full measure
of might bereft of right.
In the blue haze of distance,

Mount Baboquivari holds
a permanent stance
of knowledge and warning,
born long before the wall
and destined to remain a landmark
after desert reclaims its hideous scar.

Vulva or Mouth

in memory of Howard Zinn (1922–2010), who gave us back our history

Where sheets of water
glisten against rock,
she sits with the young girl
to speak of earlier years.
What she remembers
of her childhood,
the stories the old ones
told before they left.

He chooses the quiet of a cave
where faded handprints
linger on rock
to bring the children
his sister cannot instruct
since jaguar stilled her voice.
They must understand
who came before and how.

Later noun and verb are enhanced
by knotted string or beads,
footprints in stone,
symbols nudge memory,
images on clay pots
or pecked into canyon walls,
and those who need the stories
multiply.

Pictures or letters come together
in words, stories ring out
in amphitheaters,
numbers speak of season

and storm,
when to build or move,
cycles birthing need and desire
on the land.

Who then could imagine a time
when life would be told
by poets and historians,
painters and dancers,
each weaving the threads
to favor honor or blame,
lineage of whatever kind
in future tense.

Below the mystery figures
on the great panel
in Horseshoe Canyon
is a small reclining *V*:
vulva or mouth.
Streaming from it
a long line of people
journey through time.

Only with improvisation,
imagination and risk
can we interpret
legacy.
Only by listening
in every generation
to those who live the stories,
tell them.

Cursive Writing and Old Slide Rules

One day I will walk in a graveyard
where cursive writing and old slide rules
sleep beneath dead leaves
and rain-soaked earth.

Elaine's chortling laugh, one phrase
from a Brandenburg concerto
that once lifted my heart
above cacophony of noise

sweep anonymous streets,
shielding our human register from touch.
I may stop to pay tribute
to crinolines and cashmere sweater sets,

eggbeaters, rotary phones, transistor
radios and old typewriters,
their red and black ribbons
floating spirals

over moss-covered stones on misty nights.
I may recall an IBM Selectric,
the raised letters of its tired steel ball
glistening in the light of a waning moon.

A permanently signaling left arm
thrusts from the window of a 1941 Ford,
its upholstery smelling faintly
of burnt plush.

A 78 rpm record spins beneath
the diamond tip of a tiny needle,
recreating Patsy Cline's familiar sound
in my astonished ears.

Daughters of the American Revolution
refuse Constitution Hall
to Marian Anderson's perfect voice,
and Eleanor Roosevelt

makes it right by inviting her to sing
before Lincoln's imposing figure,
where 75,000—black and white—
hold her offended voice.

Weekly newsreels at the RKO, Superman
vanquishing Khrushchev, Walkmans
—their earplugs deafening an era—
The Joy of Cooking, first edition,

and casseroles topped with thick slices
of Velveeta cheese.
Carnation corsages dyed two-tone pink to match
a strapless prom gown lost to memory.

Where will I find one reason to nourish
the hope that tomorrow's graveyards
may imprison darker relics, dangerous
even in their afterlife:

all those advertising claims, the lies
of those we love who love us back,
our hatred of children,
and this grim currency of violence?

When will we bury greed,
erase our fear of women and difference,
trust ourselves,
design a final resting place for war?

Dare I hope noise camouflaged as ideas,
dogma or commanding truth
will one day fail to greet me
as I rise each morning

and make my stumbling way through
digital possibility,
clutch the Mohawk two-wheeler,
faint oiled skin of that first Royal portable

or your green rayon dress, Mother,
with its white rope pattern
still so comforting to my young
and trusting cheek?

The Algorithm Tells All

Who can predict this song
will top the charts,
she will keep the weight off,

our romance will live
a decade hence,
or this war will end:

all questions easily solved
in today's
measureable world.

There's an algorithm for that,
the mathematician says,
and solves the problem

using a finite sequence
of instructions.
And so the arbitrary finite

ignores the infinite: idea
to design,
design to chair,

her ashes beneath
this plum tree,
new fruit bursting

along its slender branches,
and we move from
intuition's pockmarked field

to this string of scratchings
on a chalkboard.
Scratchings to me,

but language to the experts,
nouns and verbs
and promises of relief,

quota of certainty.
I try to grasp that language
but its rules elude me.

Polls yield their numbers.
No one mentions
one sample has no women,

another ignores the homeless
or fails to consider
the gender queer

who refuses to check one
of two available boxes.
Another is funded by corporations.

We inhabit a time
when lies
masquerade as fact.

Where may I find their secrets?
Mystery shivers
at reason's edge.

Probability cannot take
community's place,
and the beating of a single heart

—animal, vegetable, or mineral—
will echo forever
through winter dark.

Truth or Dare

for Patricia Varas

Words fall short again this morning
in our game of Truth or Dare.
I pick a bruised verb from the floor,
massage her broken limbs,
whisper there will be other chances
to go for the jugular.

Cradling two offended nouns
in sorrowing palms,
I tell them humiliation is sleight of hand
and the word revolution,
though glorious in years past,
is sucked dry by fashion now.

Adjectives and adverbs
require patient nurturing,
accustomed as they are to excess
abused by the hard sell moguls
who proclaim fastest and loudest
this season's best.

Homelessness and collateral damage
huddle with wrongful death
and legitimate claim.
They rub each other's aching backs,
wipe the shame
from averted eyes.

I put them all on an exercise regime,
dress them in new courage,
remind them hope is a pendulum

swinging on strong vines
from trees
still obscuring the forest.

Who wants to hold hands
with patriotism
when it defends hate, fears love,
and will run to board
the last train of cattle cars
roaring into the station?

Expletives feel ugly or inferior
in the mouths of radio madmen
speaking for the Great White Father.
Pronouns are tired,
unsure of their usefulness
in any light.

All these words with hurt feelings
and sore joints
long for a Socrates,
Shakespeare or Sapphire
to wake them, fill them with energy,
give them their moment of meaning

in the lonely silence
crushing my breast.
They want to lead us
into the fray again.
Words: you who have lost
your courage,

I can offer you
only a light and troubled sleep.

What It Means to Belong[3]

Pawel looks in the mirror, touches
the unfamiliar bobby pin
holding his yarmulke to new curls.
Sometimes a skinhead stares back.

His mother gave him the bobby pin
and with his father broke the silence
—Poland 2010—looked away
as they told him he couldn't know

what it was like back then, every week
a new law meant to erase their lives,
those boxcars pulsing with people
like them, leaving for a place

from which there was no return.
Some of us could pass and we did.
Pawel's hand drops to his groin; he
remembers his mother's blond hair

before it greyed, the red sateen
of a childhood neckerchief,
his Pioneers troop, and later
the Pope at Warsaw's cathedral

where he assisted the priest,
stumbled through mass,
allegiances forbidden at first
then simply life as it was:

what it meant to belong.
Sand shifted beneath his feet,
burned his flesh,
and years brought new messages:

layers of the onion peeling away,
leaving him cold and alone.
When he started running
with the neighborhood gang,

when he shaved his head,
raised his arm in Nazi salute,
fear stormed his parents' cheeks
and he caught whispered half-words

at the butcher shop and library,
dreamed his grandfather's mouth
opening and closing where the mouth
of Saint Stanislaus should be.

Pawel's world spun faster, faster,
until his parents sat down one day
and told him the truth.
Sometimes the spinning unravels.

Orthodoxy makes neat piles of memory
and the pendulum
comes to a stop,
stilling its rattle of broken bones.

Evidence[4]

Sixty-five years after the defeat of horror,
twenty-nine architectural plans
for Auschwitz-Birkenau
are presented to Benjamin Netanyahu,
Prime Minister of Israel:
detailed blueprints for barracks and crematoria,
chambers where a promise of showers
brought designer death.

Meticulously initialed by Heinrich Himmler,
the sketches will be displayed
at Israel's Holocaust memorial,
one more piece of implacable evidence.
There are those who deny the Holocaust happened,
Netanyahu remarks as he receives the gift.
Let them come to Jerusalem
and look at these plans.

Let them come to Jerusalem—anyone but Palestinians,
who may not come
even for medical help,
even if they work in the city
or still hold keys to homes
their great-grandparents built
on land usurped by Biblical prophecy,
fighting every broken promise.

No blueprints of Palestinian homes
beckon the curious or devout
here or anywhere.
No memorial
keeps them under glass,
providing evidence to the world
of lives raised, shattered,
and raised again.

These descendants of Abraham
invade, usurp, lay claim
to hearts at pasture
while those others build and rebuild,
wearing the evidence in their eyes
and at the funerals of their young,
who pit hand-thrown stones
against a machinery of war.

Let those come but not these.
Let us remember but not embrace
the lives of others from this land
where checkpoints now stain olive groves.
Blueprints for murder
displayed in righteousness,
crimes drawn for all to see
but failing to open a window in the human heart.

Palenque

On the ridge looking from and down mountainsides
to the Usumacinta River and beyond,
Palenque rises through jungle in bleached stone,
spectral white etched in moist grey:
Bàak in the mouths of modern Maya.

Centuries yet no time at all have passed since our year 800,
when a great city began to melt beneath black moss,
the snakelike roots of fig trees
wrestled walls and lintels to the ground,
sealing patios built to admit interior light.

Strong profile of Pacal the Great, one hooded eye
above long, downward curve of nose
and protruding lower lip: the king for sixty-eight years
sleeping now in his Temple of Inscriptions,
rotted to bone and gold and jade.

From 583 to 604 Yohl Ik'nal—a woman—ruled
but I do not know where she rests,
no evidence of her womanness rises from these stones,
no story of continuity or rupture wets my lips
despite this burning need to know.

The Mayan zero settles into our own numerical puzzle,
their calendar dividing the year into 260 days.
They had another with 365: eighteen months of twenty days each
plus five believed unlucky.
Each a god carrying the world's weight upon its back.

Language both ideographic and phonetic,
hieroglyphs carved in sequence into stone,
each picture, person, action, or idea
tells a story, weaves a people's history
we grasp imperfectly.

We know they adorned themselves with feathers
and beads, had five thousand dances, played flutes
and trumpets fashioned of wood and clay,
moved to the resonant beat
of turtle-shell drums.

We know they ate cornmeal and black beans,
turkey and rabbit stew, chewed gum
from the leaves of the Sopadilla tree,
drank frothy cups of dark chocolate
and recorded these customs to our curiosity.

Along a narrow footpath through jungle
threatening to close once more
over careful excavation,
I move away from the great palace
with its tower: lookout or observatory,

away from secrets cleared, cleaned, studied,
deciphered and cared for by locals
as well as archaeologists from near and far,
wander into that terrain where a kingdom
remains in darkness.

From the Tablet of the Sun and Temple of the Dead Moon
I stray from familiar season, banish my own time
from consciousness, imagine nothing,
invite anything to touch my fingertips
or stop me mid-journey.

A woman and two children appear at the far end
of a footbridge. They stand perfectly still,
no questions in their eyes. No conversation
is exchanged, no connection made
before we go our disparate ways.

Xukpi or Corner Bundle

for Julio Matheu

Xukpi or Corner Bundle, Copán strains
to steady itself in earthquake country,
its plazas and palaces
dotted with archaeology students
beneath little plastic awnings.

At the southeast edge of the Mayan kingdom
in today's Honduras,
stone faces staring back at me
taste cardamom
and dream of a Chinese sea.

Perhaps it is where we stopped
to rest, astonished
by the three-dimensional glyphs
either side of these broad steps,
rising

under that arch or by this large stone foot
suddenly splicing
our line of vision,
drawing our eyes to the shadow
of figures lost to memory.

Splayed on short-cropped grass,
we settle on our backs
in a large courtyard
from where we command
a circular view:

Great-Sun First Quetzal Macaw, Jaguar Mirror
or Waterlily-Jaguar,
Head on Earth, Smoke Monkey,
and beloved Eighteen Rabbit
are only a few who ruled this city.

What temperature of air is gone,
what expectation vanished
from ruin to discovery,
your end time
to our pilgrimage?

He drove us from Guatemala City,
brought us across the border
but seemed surprised
by our invitation to enter
the place we'd come so far to see.

Oh yes, he agreed: his ancestors,
but no one had ever offered
to pay the small fee,
bring him face to face
with the color of his skin,

shape of nose, eyes on a past
they share, the stories
he'd been told
from cradle up—
wool of the same loom.

Silence. That's all
we could give each other.
Silence and this landscape
of mystery and mirror
where ghostly questions float.

Ready to Tell Almost Everything

It's still dark. We look to our feet
on this narrow path
through tropical underbrush,
howlers screaming
branch to branch.

Suddenly, high above the trees,
rising like a phantom
toward early morning light,
a pyramid lifts its shoulders
to meet our incredulity.

"At the Waterhole" in Yucatec Maya,
or "Place of the Voices"
in the words of the Itza,
Tikal is known by
the Hair Bundle glyph

on stones that tell of dynasties and wars.
The names of its rulers:
Feather Skull, Dart-Thrower Owl,
Stormy Sky, Double Bird,
Lady of Tikal, Great Jaguar Paw

and others, some gone beneath
forest canopy, moss, erosion
and time, some still prideful
on limestone stelae
and lintels of Sopadilla wood

too often taken to foreign museums
when the word *loot*
wasn't used by archaeologists
and white skin still believed
itself the favored keeper of treasure.

A giant Kapok tree, sacred to the Maya
who remain, single presence
challenging these pyramids
that soar above
a thousand shades of green.

For thirteen hundred years
—400 BC to AD 900—
one hundred thousand lived in these palaces,
played ritual ball
in these courts,

walked beneath almost constant rain,
made alliances
with the people of Copán,
and bent to the will
of Teotihuácan.

Then it was only jaguar and monkey,
grey fox, coati, toucan, eagle,
green parrot, turkey
and leafcutter ant
breaking the silence of this place.

Local people always knew
of the great stepped monuments
to a culture as majestic
as those of the Nile Valley,
Greece and Rome.

Hernán Cortés passed close in 1525
but never saw what the jungle hid,
never wrote home about a city
as great as any
praised in the worlds he knew.

Trade came and went in all directions:
one hundred thirty tons of salt alone
needed each year
to surprise the palette
or complete an ordinary table.

Rising like phantoms
but real as my breath
on its return from asthma:
relieved, revived, one step
from feisty, ready to tell

almost everything.

Man with a Crocodile Head

There's the man with a crocodile head,
dignified as all these figures are,
parading in profile
along Kom Ombo's sunlit walls,
drawing our eyes
to a life proceeding ours
by two millennia.

On the banks of the Nile, north of Aswan,
rising from steep sandstone,
dual temples to Apollo and Isis
still radiate the brilliant colors
that were their glory
when thousands worshipped
in these painted halls.

Worshipped and doctored,
for this may have been a hospital,
scalpels and forceps, scissors
and flasks of medicine
in evidence upon these walls:
a nation long wise
in the healing arts.

Doctors and patients of the Middle Kingdom
saw a crocodile in the northern sky:
their constellation
the spring-jawed reptile
speared by another hero,
his image a glyph for "collect"
or "gather together."

I want to know why Sobek, crocodile god,
is never depicted tearing his victims
limb from limb, dark bronze
of his back and dirty purple belly
dragging a man or woman
into the churning Nile waters,
green eyes snapping in hunger.

Why are these colors not embossed
upon Kom Ombo's walls?
Why does Sobek always compete
with sun god Ra,
emerging from waters of chaos
to create the world
rather than lunging for food?

Try as they will, Kom Ombo's heroic colors
cannot diminish hues of ordinary life:
Nubian farmers displaced by Lake Nasser
paint the walls of their homes
in pastel delight
as they tend their fields
of sugarcane and corn.

Teeth rip at the graceful feluccas,
reminding us of those disasters
hovering between
human cruelty to humans
and those we call natural:
so often indistinguishable
in the history we write.

Against the Weight of a Feather
for Barbara

The heart in Hallmark splendor:
red satin on its bed of paper lace
brightens cards
or holds chocolates
in little fluted trays
designed to conjure cleanliness
and salivate the tongue.

Heartfelt, heartsick, heartthrob,
all describe feelings
synonymous with love,
our very existence
if bypassing danger,
transplanting the organ
that keeps us charging forward.

In Egypt's ancient kingdoms
each dead pharaoh's heart
was carefully placed
on a scale,
weighed against a feather
to measure the substance
of his soul.

At Teotihuácan long lines of captives
high on peyote
mounted the altars
where obsidian knives
gouged their hearts and livers from living bodies.
In Mexico's museum
the altars still radiate fear.

Frida's heart dripped pain and jealousy
across her canvases,
soaking their texture in blood,
changing their molecules.
Her arteries were maps
leading us
to where she works today.

When AIDS first gripped
our community of lovers,
an artist set two ticking clocks
beside each other.
One beating heart would stop
before its counterpart,
describing the emptiness of loss.

Those who believe civilization and progress
have made us better, smarter,
more sensitive to love and tragedy,
wander a strange wilderness
where Up is Down
and ideas come candy-wrapped
in poisoned webs of shame.

If I lost touch and hearing,
belief or certainty,
I would still know
the rhythm of your heart.
Its gentle music
would still guide me
home.

Thank You

Thank you for the perfect call
of the canyon wren
and her mate's response.
For that line
where water caresses rock
rising and falling
the breadth of a canyon wall.
Thank you for explosion of birth
times four.
The portal where I disappear
into a painting by Arshile Gorky
even as I stand
on the outside looking in.
Thank you, oh, thank you
for my sleep
curled around your sleep,
your skin's temperature,
Bach's clavichord
journeying from ear to heart
and back,

its sound entering every pore,
drawing desire
into my throat.
Thank you for the grandchild's smile,
so like his father's or mother's,
but more alive.
For the day we finally win
what should have been ours
from birth
and the hope sustaining us
each time we lose.
The poem that pulls me
into the moment
instead of telling me about it.
Thank you for helping me know
there is no one to thank
but all of us
carrying memory on our shoulders,
our dead moving beside us,
whispering in our ears.

David

Death came sudden
as you drove
Placitas's back roads,
eyes moving out
across hills and ravines
in search of your beloved horses.

I see their silhouettes,
the connections you made for us:
those wild creatures
who counted you
familiar,
welcomed you close.

The mother with her colt,
young siblings sparring,
or tender touch
of two friends,
their great bodies glistening
in transparent desert light.

Now death's implacable silence
holds your generous smile,
artist's eye,
and quiet intelligence,
leaving the shattered heart
of the man you left behind

and we who strain to see
our mountain
behind its curtain
of roiling dust,
stumbling through space,
bereft of answers.

I think of you now
running with those horses,
still speaking to them
through your camera lens,
interpreting as only you could
that language we still need.

Laurette at Teotihuácan

for my son Gregory

You walk with small steps, back absolutely erect,
a picnic basket swinging on your arm.
From the painted cane of that basket
dark breads and rich pâtés emerge
along with monogrammed linen,
butter knives and a thermos of good tea.

Your weekly visit meets with local diggers
who work according to your instruction
and design, the way you contemplate
four thousand years in a perfect brown clay pot,
decide it will travel home with you
or remain among these on-site findings.

You try to explain this Palace of the Butterflies,
how ordinary houses spill their secrets,
completing a city
crowned by pyramids. Sun. Moon.
A world you see but struggle to explain
against official rhetoric.

My small son plays along the trenches,
laughs in fresh earth, runs back to us,
lured by the scent of roasted chicken
or stuffed chayote when it's time for lunch.
Beneath his blonde curls
old eyes absorb each glint and shadow.

Teotihuácan, where you offer imagination
and I begin to learn what it means
to understand too much
in a world that values tradition
and the ideas of men
over female wisdom, female risk.

In Search of the Next Sun

At Teotihuácan I watch helpless as you slip away,
are sucked, taken
from this time into that other.
You walk beside me,
children and grandchildren oblivious, scattered
between the Pyramids of Sun and Moon
along broad Avenue of the Dead,
but I know it is only your shell accompanies me,
silent and pale as chalk.

Later you try to describe the plaçe you escaped
with such effort: brittle and cold
between two millennia gone and now.
How you tore yourself from the witness
of your hologram eyes,
obsidian knife entering breast
after breast, blood-drenched hearts
lifted from darkness to sky
in search of the next sun.

Birthplace of gods, at its moment of greatest glory,
a pulsing city of pyramids
and butterfly palaces,
home to two hundred thousand Otomi, Zapotec,
Mixtec, Maya, Nahua and Totonac,
craftspeople, potters,
worshippers of Quetzalcoatl:
feathered serpent who gave them
source and ordinary life.

Something terrible happened here
was all you could say
when you finally made it back to me,
something unspeakable,
and you did not speak of it
until our poet friend
told her own near-death experience
of being caught at the pyramid's highest point,
unable to descend.

At Chaco, too, you feel the terror,
especially at Pueblo Bonito: Great House
of six hundred rooms holding central kivas
in its arms, incomplete circle
of walls, small doors and high windows
framing passing clouds to capture beauty
camouflaging what happened eight hundred years ago
when this was the center,
hub of roads stretching to cardinal winds.

And at Canyon de Chelly, Spanish bungling
of the Navajo Tsegi—"inside the rock"
where in 1805, at the place two streams converge,
a shattered cave remains as evidence.
Invaders massacred women, children, old men,
and two centuries later
their fear inhabits your body,
you draw into yourself,
the screams cutting desert air that day.

In a thousand years if we are still searching
for the next sun,
I wonder if certain visitors to Auschwitz,
Ramallah, Baghdad, Kabul, Soweto,
Morazán, Acteal, or Port-au-Prince
may feel themselves pulled into a dimension
between their time and ours, fear
they will not escape
what we still do to one another.

Underground Astronomy

In this Place of the House of Flowers
now known as Xochicalco,
where twenty thousand once worshipped
at a Temple of the Feathered Serpent,
played ritual ball, sweated in baths
built to cleanse, and welcomed artists
from other parts of Mesoamerica,
some in surrounding villages
still speak Nahuatl.

I am drawn by the asymmetrical angles
of curved levels
threading beyond the picture plane
through giant trees,
their careful rock terraces
so different from
the balance I have seen
in other ancient sites
across this land.

Could this have been the first
artists' community of the Americas?
Carvers and painters
plastered a cave
black, yellow, and red,
cut the slant of its chimney
hexagonal above,
8.7 meters to where it opens
to let a traveling sun stream through.

On its implacable journey toward Cancer,
one hundred five days from April 30th
to August 15th, searing rays
penetrate a narrow opening,
project themselves on the stone floor:
no tower but underground astronomy
erasing flesh, leaving
only the bones of my trembling hand
glowing red in this shaft of light.

Keeper of Art and Laughter
for my daughter Sarah

South from Chaco's broad canyon
and Paquimé's soft adobe,
a plumb line swings from the sun:
longitude and latitude
coming together in places
destined for community.

Los Guachimontones on Jalisco's plain,
shadowed by Volcán de Tequila,
lines of maguey ribbing gentle hills:
pulque for Teuchitlán's dark *expendios*,
where a wooden ladle in a clay vat
is still a 50-*centavo* drink.

Ehecatl—god of wind—watches
over ten circular complexes,
stepped pyramids
rising in layers,
missing only the wooden platforms
where the *voladores* once raised

ladders and eighty-foot poles,
climbed to the sky,
then descended head down,
arms outstretched to Quetzalcoatl:
god of the morning star,
keeper of art and laughter.

Lone visitors, we leave our car
in the empty lot,
its freshly-painted divider lines
gleaming midday yellow,
the strange pyramids
visible beyond a ridge of trees.

A half-dozen guides lean idle
against a wooden shack,
sipping bright orange Fanta
from recycled bottles.
One offers to show us around
and we follow her in.

Conclusion: this is the missing piece,
mortar linking civilizations
north to south and
south to north.
Yet no one knows much
about the people

who built these pyramids,
lived here two thousand years ago,
played ball on these two vast courts,
fashioned the obsidian tools
and clay figurines on display
at Guadalajara's new museum.

My daughter Sarah and her partner
walk ahead, hand in hand.
Grandsons Sébas and Juan
are on their knees,
shaping loose earth
into little round pyramids of their own.

I dream of coordinates, numbers
that may tell me how straight the line,
how precise the spot
where maguey reaches for cloud
and *voladora* ghosts vanish
before they come to earth.

Frida's Column

for my daughter Ximena

"To hope, with anguish restrained,
the broken column . . . moving
my life created of steel."
—*Frida Kahlo's diary*

Emerging from surgery in 1944,
Frida paints herself a broken column,
stares back from this canvas,
corseted and confined.

Her face is sown with tears
but she does not cry.
Spikes protrude from her body
but no blood comes.

Dark nipples adorn perfect breasts,
nipples of motherhood
though this woman
will never bear a child.

Her single brow lifts like a bird.
Her hair is loose and wild.
No combs, no ribbons,
no flowers.

Standing before a landscape
of desert ochre and purple sky,
her hips are loosely wound
in a Christlike shroud.

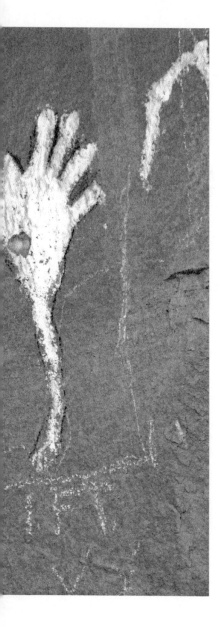

It's the shattered Ionic column
pulls our eye to that place
where vertebrae should ridge
beneath her skin,

that column propping soft flesh
of a body destroyed by accident
and doctors, holding it erect
from loin to stoic head.

Upon that column her chin rests
between defiant and resigned.
Her cold calm
poses only the question

with no answer,
the last dilemma
to which all evidence
responds.

Hermes, Shapeshifter
for Barrett Price and Raymond Suttner

Liminal space: threshold between Here and There,
even when Here retreats
into the silver-grey of early morning light
and There turns her back
as you reach to grab her hand.

Not prison or torture, homelessness
or hunger,
not the pointed shape of pain
but amorphous fear of what's to come,
unknowable and waiting.

Shadow that might have been definition
in a different time,
sound stuttering to silence
along these walls,
mute testament to earlier lives.

Hermes, shapeshifter, he of the winged shoes,
patron of boundaries,
who cares alike
for liars and poets,
protects old crones and young whores.

Underworld messenger, bringer of dreams,
who deals in weights and measures,
keeps his eye on injured athletes,
travelers Here no longer
yet never arriving There.

Because he lay with Chione
the same night
she took another lover,
Hermes slips between tectonic plates,
balancing a present that disappears

and a future never quite brought to focus,
pulls us
between one last burst of rage
and the perfect halves
of this geode opening to our touch.

Coming from Nothing, Going to Nothing

Climbing above Ollantaytambo's narrow lanes,
we return to a day in 1475 when Inca arrived
at the confluence of Patakancha and Urubamba,
what's left of Huáscar's fight with Atahualpa,
warring through the centuries.

Little plastic flags signal each block's dwelling,
where locals drink from chicha vats
and small boys squat to defecate in courtyards
filled with garbage, iron-age tools,
and scampering *cuy*.

We pass the shop where a poncho in tones
of grey and brown becomes Earth itself,
past the single man with his flute,
playing for visitors or his own heart,
climb endless terraced steps

into air barely holding up its end of the bargain,
mocking our lungs as we gasp and climb
high enough to view the ancient granaries,
stone ledges against a green so dark and dense,
it is only at home in this latitude of mountain.

That's where they stored three hundred varieties
of potato, maize, squash, beans, quinoa,
manioc and coca leaves
still caressing my tongue
against the lean years.

We struggle to decipher their high windows
in such transparent air,
move up and farther
until we reach the six great capstones,
enormous slabs of rock

brought here without machine or wheel,
impossible to imagine hauling them
then or now across the churning river
and unforgiving terrain
from quarries five kilometers distant.

A simple pattern stares back at me where
tonnage on tonnage rarely includes
such messages on stone—
geometric slide of steps
etched along one side of the giant centerpiece:

Coming from nothing, going to nothing,
you say, confident we will understand
complexity in this simplest of designs.
The answer to a single question
trembling in air too scant to close my mouth.

Yes, I manage: *Coming from nothing,
going to nothing.* I have always known
this truth—stripped of that poor vanity
invented to dumb the searching mind—
is the only truth there is.

The man with his flute has followed us
to the top. Still plays.
Below, oblivious to visitors,
only field and stone, silence and echo
as far as the ear can see.

We Are Hungry
for my grandson Daniel

We are hungry

so, voracious for profit,
you feed us malignant seed,
process our food
to chemical poison
until mutation claims our children
and our children's children.

We are sick

so you check us against
preexisting conditions,
sell us hyped pills
guaranteed to make you rich,
and their side effects
override our body's wisdom.

We are cold

so you publish feature stories
about our tent cities
and build more shelters
even as your banks
take back the homes
you made us buy.

We wonder

so you give us religion and politics,
systems rigged
to keep us following a leader
while our beautiful minds
wither and rot,
subservient to power.

We want to learn

so you ply us with information,
misinformation,
distortion and discipline,
test and rearrange our scores,
discourage questions,
punish thought.

We are forced to wander

in endless migration
from those places
where old stories
caress our skin
to others where cast-off rhythms
change the weight of bones.

We ask questions

so you smile and tell us
not to worry, leave it
to the experts,
it's too complicated
for ordinary folk to understand.
Just trust us, you say.

We are afraid

so you pit us against one another,
recruit us to holy wars
fought in your lust for conquest
and to do away with those
who challenge
your crimes.

We are desperate

so you close down those places
where promise of solace lives
and put us to pasture,
lock us in prisons
privatized to your profit
and our despair.

We age

so you speak not to but about us,
offer us fast food,
diet pills, silicone, Botox,
then hide us in nursing homes
camouflaged by the sugar scent
of death.

Despite your criminal games
and calculated risk,
we do remember
Lilith and Socrates,
Ghandi, Rosa Parks,
King, Mandela,
Aung San Suu Kyi,
Audre Lorde,
and the youngest child
struggling to create
one more morning of life.

Peeling the Onion
for Sam Menefee-Liby

Miguel Hernández and his onion
flash before me,
his lonely prison cell.

Spain's fading war we learn
was good
despite dead poets, lingering loss.

The young man tossing this onion
into my sea of questions
says he was 14

when the planes hit the towers,
billowing smoke repeated
across our TV screens,

says his coming of age was shaped
by its aftermath, how we
as a nation answered hate with hate.

He says this—or maybe it's me—
fills in the blanks
between image and meaning.

The onion is in my hands, its raw skin
stings my eyes.
He wants me to peel it back,

find that moment when history
might have righted itself
and we could have chosen

another path, turned it around,
held a future
we cannot find today.

He asks when it went wrong,
where we met
the wall of no return.

Memory ricochets inside my skull.
I am older than old,
my infant self

tumbling head-on toward me,
threatening balance
and trusted maps.

Onions always make me cry.
I peel layer after layer,
discard the papery inner core.

He is not asking where we failed
or what went wrong
but when. I hear myself answer

Vietnam. McCarthy. Cold War politics
or before. Manifest Destiny.
The Middle Passage. Dirty blankets.

Those who came from the east
looking for freedom,
destroying the freedom of others.

Those who came from the south
with gunpowder and Cross,
looking for gold on a desert clad in sun.

The walls keeping Out and In,
the fences forever cutting
a people off from itself.

The onion peels until nothing is left.
My tears dry. Where do we go
when memory sleeps?

Give a man a gun, the soldier said,
and chances are
he won't kill easily.

You have to teach a man to kill.
And when you do,
how do you teach him to stop?

Real Books

for my brother John

Thailand's Ayutthaya: serene Buddhas
and sky-piercing stupas burnt to ashen heat.
Jerash's free-standing columns
leaning in on one another
against a sky of cobalt blue—I am on my back
looking up. Pale shapes of Champa temples in rain:
a culture we forget when we say Vietnam.
The Ephesus library, nothing but facade
to those who cannot read its stone.

Chichén's great ball court still thunders
with echo of ritual games.
Petra's rose-red rock and tired camels.
Tulum's tiny beach: scene of such
loading and unloading, undersea tunnels
guarding secrets in both directions.
Cobá, buried beneath jungle.
El Tajín with its hundreds of niches,
empty of all but memory.

Stone books: I read your pages clear as paper,
covered in words familiar to my tongue
or not. Whether language comes
in pictures, glyphs, script, beads, knots,
printed or painted by the artist's hand,
whether I can mimic diphthongs and clicks,
absorb its silence, decipher its whisper,
ruins bid me sit awhile, pulling story
from shape of window, width of door.

We live on the threshold of another shift
in knowledge transmission—walls
to stone tablets, papyrus beaten to receive
its letters, illuminated parchment
to hand-printed tomes, hardcover to paperback—
books have gone electronic now:
two hundred titles on your Kindle,
random assortment in a device so small
you might confuse it with a postage stamp.

They say cyberspace will bring us together,
equalize and unify, give rich and poor
the same tools to call opportunity
back from precipice.
One laptop per child, cybercafés
on every street in a Global Village,
everyone communicating instantly
as class and race and gender
cower beneath voracious fingertips.

I say listen to the message these ruins
carry through millennia,
what distances and final solutions
mean for real people speaking words
that mirror longing, sorrow, joy.
What we feel, what we know
of the feelings of others:
what keeps us human,
face to face and page to page.

Ars Poetica

A poem isn't made of angst;
the poet takes aim
at person, place, event
or feeling:
one of those intangibles
mocked by keepers of the realm,
academy, imprisoned sensibility.

A poem must pull its audience
from comfort, apathy,
the dulling din of nine to five
or dusk to dawn,
surprise us in midstep,
confound all held assumptions
and drop us upside down in Wonderland.

Alice was afraid but kept on going,
pushing the limits
of perception.
We are never closer to the answer
than when we touch our age's coldest edge
or lose ourselves
in the volcano's molten roar.

Last Poem

1.

Born into love and stagecraft, deception dressed
in exception and impeccable taste,
even as you trembled, confident of success,
you saw what was there, took all of it in,
every wrinkle and scar,
assumed it would always be yours,
never crumble at your touch.

Later you believed you saw more than others,
eyes boring through animal vegetable mineral,
architecture of meaning with every frame
a falling domino, secret vibrato of radio waves
feeding the common good.
Inherited superiority
though you could not have understood that then.

2.

Lines on your map led to hidden places where
you alone could see beyond the ridge
into the next valley and the next.
Where you journeyed, others followed
and you attached yourself
to courage, creative change
under any spotlight.

Sometimes she had a name, a line
where river cuts through rock
and keeps on carving,
time bends to rebellious rhythm.
Musical notes you never quite heard
since designated tone-deaf
in a family of Friday night quartets.

3.
And there were other traumas: she doesn't
like dogs, people said, never asking why,
who used her and when,
who built that bridge of shame.
Or the mushrooms whose very image
made her sick and watchful, forever alert
against the threat for which no memory remained.

Always a quiver of danger shrouding
the slow-blooming flower,
years dipping your fingers in invisible ink
as if what couldn't be seen
wouldn't be counted or take up space
on the register of common events
ticking on every clock.

4.
I became *we*, singular plural
in your lexicon of longing.
Children climbed on your shoulders,
yours and the progeny of others,
their endless migrations pinning you to Earth,
enormous eyes, small limbs, dry mouths
spitting nothing but raucous hope.

All those times you thought you had found
The One: too many by society's rules,
and it wasn't that hard to walk away
when no compromise could heal, no fix
replenish the liquid of possibility.
You were never alone so alone was better
than clinging to one who cut you down.

5.

Four imaginary childhood friends morphed
into the brilliant artist tracing her own map,
then into the revolutionary whose words
promised justice for all until you noticed
his *all* excluded those you loved,
discovered layers of rigged complexity
are always inventions of abuse.

After all those lives and lies you were free
to look from your own eyes,
see the woman who waited,
juggling trust like a burning wire.
Slowly she opened until both of you knew
the secret is going more than all the way,
more than the sum of its parts.

6.

It is here in this crevice of ancient rock,
outside wind and temperature
inside what was never supposed to happen
you find the polished stone,
new words sear the palms of your hands.
The few years left shine
brighter than those gone by.

Just the right amount: wild and raw,
all scores settled,
a breath for every flute.

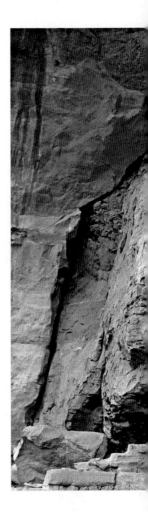

Socrates Walks Barefoot

I follow trudging crowds up Acropolis hill,
where scaffolding scars stone
but awe still has its finger in my eye.
I linger before a partial frieze
then move to an almost-perfect capital,

follow its column down to rubble of stone—
a line of script, first century BC echo
anchoring twenty-first century candy wrapper
and half-empty Coke can
someone has left on this low wall.

The laws of one, three, five, seven, nine,
pentagram and other male signs
fade momentarily. The laws of two,
four, six, eight embrace me:
polarity, duality, resolution.

Women strike balance. Sparta's Neolithic goddess
lives in the heft of these round thighs.
A Minoan woman bends over pendulous breasts
two thousand years before men's war
reduces her to frescos on a wall.

The caryatids overlook a city synonymous
with all of Western culture,
Golden Proportion forever.
Delphi's oracle rides the wind and aging widows
hawk blue charms against the evil eye.

Despite such female abundance, what pierces me
to the column of my being
is Socrates walking barefoot through the Agora below,
engaged in conversation no hemlock could kill.
Today's child asks a question.

Another question responds.

Perga Rests Its Broken Bones
for Behlul Dundar

East of Antalya's jigsaw old and new,
Hadrian's Gate stitches wooden houses
to steel and glass of modern urbanity.
Perga rests its broken bones.
Great theater and Olympic stadium
both empty, colonnades and streets
swept clean, ornate lintels
resting on the ground.

She knows but is silent, waiting
for the moment words may help
instead of hurt. A trading city
twenty kilometers from shore,
perfect defense two thousand years ago
when pirate bands less desperate
than today attacked that stretch
of Mediterranean coast.

Ceramic pipes at the Roman baths
seem ready to wash my thirsty skin.
Defiant green pushes from mosaic floors,
embraces what's left of another set
of twin towers, a fallen entranceway.
The agora displays neat shops
empty now
of all but its most persistent ghosts.

Alexander the Great was here in 333 BC
—a year as ordinary as heroic—
but it's Apollonius
whispers mathematical figures to my ear:
circles, ellipses, parabolas
and hyperbolae all shooting stars
to solutions Ptolemy and Kepler
discover in a future yet to come.

Ephesus wins most of the poster space,
basks in the glow of this nation
straddling continents, offering
Cappadocia's painted caves,
an energy of whirling semazens,
and Rumi's poems: pure and elegant
beneath a mob of devotees
moving through Konya's daunting shrine.

Dignity of a Hittite water temple
and ruins of caravanserai
spaced in perfect welcome
to travelers of another time,
spice markets and the hundreds
of working wells dotting farmlands
that claim their poppy seeds
are only for sweet morning bread.

Perga stretches and decides to speak
when I reach out to touch its stone.
When I am listening.

Separating Aspendos from Sky

Against this elaborate facade, the platform
where masked dancers once performed
is covered with plastic,
music stands arranged
in orchestral configuration,
a woman in dark glasses
and bright green dress
finishes the sound check,
exits stage left.

Thirty tan and white feral cats
chase in and out of supports
made to simulate ancient stone.
Outside, an eager young man
squeezes fresh oranges
into tiny plastic cups
and bored camels adorned
with weaves of beaded headgear
pose with tourists for a lira or two.

Since mid-second century,
this great two-tiered fan
of stepped seats rises steep
to its cap of graceful arches
separating Aspendos from sky:
cerulean blue, dotted today
with little puffed clouds
lingering postcard perfect
in my eyes.

String quartets, opera, and ballet
play to rave reviews,
bringing visitors each year
to this theater's seven thousand seats.
But in ancient drama
the gods spoke,
demanded that lives change.
Can modern symphonic strains
better that thunder of old?

Where the Dead Lived Better than the Living

Hidden for centuries behind a cleft of rock
in this broad valley
between the Dead Sea and Gulf of Aqaba,

called Thamud in the Qur'an
and known by other names
in mouths of Bedouins through brittle desert time,

the narrow Siq opens and we emerge, astonished
by Al Khazneh, facade of red-rose rock
they call The Treasury.

Petra's tombs, towering, magnificent
and simple living caves
unfold along Mount Hor's ravines.

Jebal al-Madhbah's High Place of Sacrifice
looks upon a landscape still draining blood
from the ghosts of goats and camels.

Two thousand seven hundred years ago
Nabataeans greeted
the Silk Road caravans

with currency of water: clay conduits,
snaking stone, masterful dams and cisterns
warming desert's harsh terrain.

Arab legend gives us Moses striking rock
with his staff
and the peace-keeping liquid gushing forth.

Caravans came from Gaza, Alexandria,
Al-Hijr, the Negev and Sinai,
as far as the Red Sea and beyond,

brought cooking oil and medicine, copper,
beauty powders and creams for the living,
bitumen to embalm the dead.

Egyptians, Greeks, Romans, even Christians
layered their cultures
at this crossroads of desert-dwellers and travelers

where the dead lived better than the living,
and tired donkeys bear tourists today,
flies buzz the ears of gaunt horses,

and men hawk coins that may be old
or made to look as if they are.
Village signs scream *Indiana Jones*

and someone's uncle with millennial dignity
offers us conversation
and silver-seated glasses of sweet tea.

The Bedouins living for generations
in these caves
are unimpressed with the cement boxes

their government has built on that far hill.
It is impossible
to imagine the throb of ancient metropolis

in the vacant eyes of palaces and tombs.
Too much of a disconnect.
Too out of sync with time.

Different on the Family Farm

In ancient communities
farmers kept their seed
generation to generation,

put real food in their bodies,
fed their animals, ate
to live and keep illness away.

Along the Nile River,
Africa's Great Rift Valley,
throughout the Mayan kingdom,

in Uxmal's backyard,
and these canyons I call home,
the milpa was sustenance.

Rice sprouted tall
in the Mekong's waters,
wheat awoke as bread.

Those not killed by war
die poisoned today
in the spirit of free enterprise.

It was different at Palenque
and Kom Ombo. It was different
on the American family farm, 1932.

Grateful Without Knowing Why

Large black bird, insistent in its repetitive caw,
lifts the shade on day.
Sweet trill of smaller wings—its counterpoint—
though you find no need
to name their back and forth.

Swoosh of breeze in branches, howl of wind
through canyons,
beat of rain and slow drip of water
seeping from fern-covered spring
at the back of your cave.

Ice cracking and shattering stone,
macaw voice and turkey cackle
interrupting the ghosts
who whisper to your sleep.
Dream time and sound time.

Silence also has its place in this concert,
embracing ear and memory.
Long silence and short.
You think of this as you breathe
faster and slower through one long night.

Obsidian knife hollows a flute, carves holes
where practice asks fingers
to squeeze and release as you blow out,
reach the end of breath
and blow again.

Someone stretches skin over the mouth
of a pot broken in fire,
fastens it with strips
from the same pelt,
discovers resonance.

Unplanned but rapturous, this duet
of lips and fingers,
the heel of the other's hand:
joined passions keeping time
with breath.

Music enters these canyons.
Your people
but also Bach, Makeba, Thelonious,
Bartoli and Dylan
are grateful without knowing why.

The Magic in What We Know

"Drawing . . . brings together [humans]
and the world. It lives through magic."
—Keith Haring, *Journals*

He painted in subways and on walls,
at first uninvited, then to applause,
loved children and died of AIDS at 31.

Radiant Child glyph or *Barking Dog*
before a TV monitor
blaring greed and war.

Lineage glyphs on the stelae at Copán,
bull in docility or rage
in the glyphs of ancient Egypt.

The man or woman who chiseled the birth scene
and stylized snake
onto two sides of a boulder outside Moab,

the nomad who pecked two perfect feet
on a canyon wall in Jordan's Wadi Rum
also drew for others.

Lines we receive through this lens
called progress,
intention and meaning escape the cultivated eye.

Haring was right millennia ago
and in our market-driven now:
the artist's line connects us to identity,

defines the magic we hold
in open hands.

Blood Lightning Speaks⁵

1.

In Nebaj we pass through streets
where sleepwalking ghosts walk,
answering our questions
in tongues we don't understand
or staring silently.

A torturous climb past cemetery
of pastel afterlife,
sudden waterfall around a bend,
then into this humid village
where time measures differently,

dead and living spirits cross paths
in broad daylight
as if they are one and the same,
avoiding our eyes
while making themselves at home.

A great migration of Swainson's Hawks
fly north each spring,
torol k'älaj or bringers of rain,
lifting the Southern Cross
from sea.

As distant from Nebaj
as those who delivered fresh fish
to Machu Picchu's royalty
centuries ago and latitudes away
where another empire sang.

Each fall the hawks fly south again,
dropping the Southern Cross
below horizon's line,
clearing the rains
and bringing seed to furrow.

Torol sak'j, the constellation
announcing the dry season,
is not the same Southern Cross
of vernal sky
I've searched these seventy years

but a splatter of stars called *sigma, phi,*
delta, gamma, lambda, epsilon, and *eta*
in our Western rendering,
xic or hawk
in the K'iche' noun-verb

of the highland Maya: my Sagittarius
moving as those birds move
in predictable return,
heralding a sky,
sweeping its rush of tears

and announcing a time to reap,
naming the day
and doing its deeds
by the short calendar[6]
with its seasonal adjustments.

Between each row of corn,
black beans and squash
turn their faces skyward,
content to follow
the tall stalks' genuflection.

Women whose cycles match corn
give birth
in the same nine months
it takes the tender plant
to ready itself for cutting.

Child and corn arrive at fruition
on the repeated day-names
of their conception or planting,
closing the circle,
keeping their histories alive.

The day keeper determines his dates
by divining moons.
Midwives note when the blood
of pregnant women
pauses to catch its breath.

The waning moon becomes *katit*,
our grandmother,
reflected when an eclipse
swims on the surface of water
set out in little pails.
Harvesting, butchering, felling trees
and having sex: all are shunned
during diminishing moons
when animals, crops, and people
are vulnerable.

Babies conceived beneath lunar wholeness
or during a partial eclipse
may be twins or transsexuals,
inseparables or two-spirit beings
changing back and forth

every three or four days, then
three or four years,
their behavior, dress
and personhood
drawn to celestial reason.

Sowing dried kernels of maize
and strong black beans
from last season
are tasks only right
for a waxing moon.

2.
Beneath Nebaj's mute surface
you, my love,
find children who lead us
to their mother: trust
taking our hands.

In this welcoming home,
open sewerage elicits the look
that passes between us.
Our host smiles, says she
understands if we're not hungry,

and we eat with urgency and shame,
breaking silence, trading lives
to the rhythm of homemade *sopa*
and threads of the huipil
telling a story we cannot read.

Blood lightning speaks and stars dip
to that mindful sea
as great kettles of hawks funnel south
and each stalk of corn
turns to its left and bows.

Keeping up with the sun, stalks rise,
guided by stars and birds:
cause and effect interchangeable
in a place where sky instructs
and time holds past and future

in a single breath.

Landscape of Possibility

Your memory moves sure-footed from old trees
to tender shoots, struggles through dry years,
robust but watchful in the wet,

travels in reed boats to a triangle of volcanic land,
where you carve great monoliths of rock
and raise them like sentinels.

It honors weather and place, nurtures cyclical ritual,
keeping sun and moon aloft,
traces hunger and plenty,

carves genealogies in stone, acknowledges lineage
so we may know who shared such experience
and what they bequeath to us.

Our memory places its footprint on the moon,
looks upon earth from a point
beyond the pull of personal gravity,

loses itself along twisted pathways of deception,
speaks a language unknown to our siblings
on the other side of the mountain,

trips over cell phones and payday loans, hidden fees,
foods murdered by pesticides,
bloated with hormones,

betrayal of animals kept in the dark and so weak
they cannot stand. Cybertriggers leave us
longing for that lost line to the night sky.

Our experts impose their memory on you,
draw what they see in black lines fading to grey
or dotted to extend the visual evidence:

where they believe you went and why,
give you names bereft of your lived lives,
their prisms of disbelief.

My neighbor cannot speak to me or hold my hand,
but your memory rises to kiss my sundried lips
and I reach back

through stone and a rain of stars,
let stillness calm my wings, silence turn me
toward a landscape of possibility.

∽ NOTES

1. Teotihuácan has most often been written Teotihuacán. Years ago, when I lived in Mexico and knew anthropologists who worked at the site, I remember hearing it pronounced with the accent on the first *a*. In the context of working on these poems, I did some research on the Nahuatl language, which reinforced my early audio information. I believe placing the accent on the first *a* may more closely approximate the original pronunciation. I have chosen, then, to render it this way throughout this book.

2. Some of the background for this poem came from "A Rich History of Chocolate in North America," by Sara Coelho, in *Science Now*, February 2, 2010. Patricia Crown, at the University of New Mexico, has been studying Chaco's cylinder vases for the better part of a decade; she discovered the Theobromine traces in the one-thousand-year-old pots.

3. Inspired by the article "Changing Face in Poland: Skinhead Puts on Skullcap" by Dan Bilefsky, *New York Times*, February 27, 2010.

4. Based on information in "Auschwitz Blueprints Given to Israeli PM" by the Associated Press, datelined Berlin and published in the *New York Times*, August 27, 2009.

5. Mayan day keepers or diviners interpret life according to mathematical calculations, using millennial teachings, calendars, positions of celestial bodies, weather, and other factors. According to anthropologist Barbara Tedlock, herself an initiated day keeper, "speaking of the blood" (*cacha' uquiqe'el*) is caused by the rapid movement of lightning within the blood and muscles of diviners. Blood lightning is the blood sending signals, or speaking.

6. The Maya base much of their reckoning on a complex system of calendars, including one that has come to be known as "the long count," stretching into an almost infinite past. Among these, there is one of 365 days and another of 260. This latter is often called "the short calendar" and is the most relevant to the way they link human, animal, and vegetable life cycles with the movements of the cosmos and agricultural seasons. The Maya pay great attention to the cycles of the moon, and their 260-day calendar allows for climate- and weather-related correction, much as the moment of conception dated by the cessation of a woman's menstrual cycle allows for corrections that make it possible to determine the date of birth with some precision.

ᔡ PHOTOGRAPHS

RUINS

Design and composition: Karen Mazur
Typeset using Bulmer MT with Copperplate Gothic display.
Printed by IBT Global, Troy, New York.